# CAMPFIRE COOKBOOK

MAIN COURSE - Breakfast, Lunch, Dinner and Dessert Recipes for Cooking outdoors

# TABLE OF CONTENTS

*BREAKFAST* ................................................................................. 7
BLUEBERRY PANCAKES .............................................................. 7
GOOSEBERRIES PANCAKES ........................................................ 9
BANANA PANCAKES ................................................................. 11
PEANUT BUTTER PANCAKES .................................................... 13
PANCAKES ................................................................................ 15
PUMPKIN MUFFINS .................................................................. 16
BANANA MUFFINS ................................................................... 18
KIWI MUFFINS .......................................................................... 20
STRAWBERRY MUFFINS ........................................................... 22
CRANBERRIES MUFFINS ........................................................... 24
MUFFINS ................................................................................... 26
CABBAGE OMELETTE ............................................................... 28
ZUCCHINI OMELETTE ............................................................... 30
ROMAINE LETTUCE OMELETTE ............................................... 32
MUSHROOM OMELETTE ......................................................... 34
LEEK OMELETTE ....................................................................... 36
COCONUT CEREAL ................................................................... 38
ZUCCHINI BREAD ..................................................................... 40
BAKED EGGS WITH ONIONS .................................................... 42
MORNING LOADED SWEET POTATO ...................................... 44
*LUNCH* ...................................................................................... 47
ASPARAGUS FRITATTA ............................................................. 47
FETA CHEESE SALAD DRESSING .............................................. 49
BRUSSELS SPROUT SALAD ....................................................... 50

| | |
|---|---|
| POTATO SALAD | 51 |
| CRANBERRY SALAD | 52 |
| PEA AND LENTIL SALAD | 53 |
| CHICKEN AND FIG SALAD | 54 |
| BABY CARROT SALAD | 55 |
| MUSHROOM & FENNEL SALAD | 57 |
| GREEN BEAN SALAD | 58 |
| WATERCRESS AND PEAR SALAD | 59 |
| WATERCRESS FRITATTA | 60 |
| KALE FRITATTA | 62 |
| TOMATO FRITATTA | 64 |
| BROCCOLI FRITATTA | 66 |
| MEDITERRANENA BUDDA BOWL | 68 |
| VEGAN CURRY | 70 |
| CAULIFLOWER WITH ROSEMARY | 72 |
| BRUSSELS SPROUTS | 73 |
| MOROCCAN STIR FRY | 75 |
| ***DINNER*** | 78 |
| SIMPLE PIZZA RECIPE | 78 |
| ZUCCHINI PIZZA | 80 |
| CAULIFLOWER RECIPE | 81 |
| BROCCOLI RECIPE | 82 |
| TOMATOES & HAM PIZZA | 83 |
| LEEK SOUP | 85 |
| ZUCCHINI SOUP | 87 |
| RUTABAGA SOUP | 89 |

CARROT SOUP ................................................................... 91

YAMS SOUP ...................................................................... 93

***SMOOTHIES*** .................................................................... 96

TANGERINE SMOOTHIE ................................................... 96

PEANUT BUTTER SMOOTHIE .............................................. 97

CARROT SMOOTHIE .......................................................... 98

GINGER SMOOTHIE ........................................................... 99

KALE SMOOTHIE ............................................................. 100

MANGO SMOOTHIE ......................................................... 101

CHIA SMOOTHIE ............................................................. 102

CRANBERRY SMOOTHIE .................................................. 103

PINEAPPLE & SPINACH SMOOTHIE ................................... 104

BLUEBERRY SMOOTHIE ................................................... 105

Copyright 2019 by Noah Jerris - All rights reserved.

This document is geared towards providing exact and reliable information in regards to the topic and issue covered. The publication is sold with the idea that the publisher is not required to render accounting, officially permitted, or otherwise, qualified services. If advice is necessary, legal or professional, a practiced individual in the profession should be ordered.

- From a Declaration of Principles which was accepted and approved equally by a Committee of the American Bar Association and a Committee of Publishers and Associations.

In no way is it legal to reproduce, duplicate, or transmit any part of this document in either electronic means or in printed format. Recording of this publication is strictly prohibited and any storage of this document is not allowed unless with written permission from the publisher. All rights reserved.

The information provided herein is stated to be truthful and consistent, in that any liability, in terms of inattention or otherwise, by any usage or abuse of any policies, processes, or directions contained within is the solitary and utter responsibility of the recipient reader. Under no circumstances will any legal responsibility or blame be held against the publisher for any reparation, damages, or monetary loss due to the information herein, either directly or indirectly.

Respective authors own all copyrights not held by the publisher.

The information herein is offered for informational

purposes solely, and is universal as so. The presentation of the information is without contract or any type of guarantee assurance.

The trademarks that are used are without any consent, and the publication of the trademark is without permission or backing by the trademark owner. All trademarks and brands within this book are for clarifying purposes only and are the owned by the owners themselves, not affiliated with this document.

Introduction

Campfire recipes for personal enjoyment but also for family enjoyment. You will love them for sure for how easy it is to prepare them.

## *BREAKFAST*

## BLUEBERRY PANCAKES

Serves: **4**

Prep Time: **10** Minutes

Cook Time: **20** Minutes

Total Time: **30** Minutes

### INGREDIENTS

- 1 cup whole wheat flour
- ¼ tsp baking soda
- ¼ tsp baking powder
- 1 cup blueberries
- 2 eggs
- 1 cup milk

### DIRECTIONS

1. In a bowl combine all ingredients together and mix well
2. In a skillet heat olive oil

3. Pour ¼ of the batter and cook each pancake for 1-2 minutes per side
4. When ready remove from heat and serve

# GOOSEBERRIES PANCAKES

Serves: **4**

Prep Time: **10** Minutes

Cook Time: **30** Minutes

Total Time: **40** Minutes

### INGREDIENTS

- 1 cup whole wheat flour
- ¼ tsp baking soda
- ¼ tsp baking powder
- 1 cup gooseberries
- 2 eggs
- 1 cup milk

### DIRECTIONS

1. In a bowl combine all ingredients together and mix well
2. In a skillet heat olive oil
3. Pour ¼ of the batter and cook each pancake for 1-2 minutes per side

4. When ready remove from heat and serve

# BANANA PANCAKES

Serves: **4**
Prep Time: **10** Minutes
Cook Time: **20** Minutes
Total Time: **30** Minutes

### INGREDIENTS

- 1 cup whole wheat flour
- ¼ tsp baking soda
- ¼ tsp baking powder
- 1 cup mashed banana
- 2 eggs
- 1 cup milk

### DIRECTIONS

1. In a bowl combine all ingredients together and mix well
2. In a skillet heat olive oil
3. Pour ¼ of the batter and cook each pancake for 1-2 minutes per side

4. **When ready remove from heat and serve**

# PEANUT BUTTER PANCAKES

Serves: **4**
Prep Time: **10** Minutes
Cook Time: **20** Minutes
Total Time: **30** Minutes

## INGREDIENTS

- 1 cup whole wheat flour
- ¼ tsp baking soda
- ¼ tsp baking powder
- 2 tablespoons peanut butter
- 2 eggs
- 1 cup milk

## DIRECTIONS

1. In a bowl combine all ingredients together and mix well
2. In a skillet heat olive oil
3. Pour ¼ of the batter and cook each pancake for 1-2 minutes per side

**4. When ready remove from heat and serve**

## PANCAKES

Serves: **4**
Prep Time: **10** Minutes
Cook Time: **30** Minutes
Total Time: **40** Minutes

### INGREDIENTS

- 1 cup whole wheat flour
- ¼ tsp baking soda
- ¼ tsp baking powder
- 2 eggs
- 1 cup milk

### DIRECTIONS

1. In a bowl combine all ingredients together and mix well
2. In a skillet heat olive oil
3. Pour ¼ of the batter and cook each pancake for 1-2 minutes per side
4. When ready remove from heat and serve

## PUMPKIN MUFFINS

Serves:         *8-12*
Prep Time:   *10*   Minutes
Cook Time:  *20*   Minutes
Total Time:  *30*   Minutes

### INGREDIENTS

- 2 eggs
- 1 tablespoon olive oil
- 1 cup milk
- 2 cups whole wheat flour
- 1 tsp baking soda
- ¼ tsp baking soda
- 1 cup pumpkin puree
- 1 tsp cinnamon
- ¼ cup molasses

### DIRECTIONS

1. In a bowl combine all dry ingredients
2. In another bowl combine all dry ingredients

3. Combine wet and dry ingredients together
4. Pour mixture into 8-12 prepared muffin cups, fill 2/3 of the cups
5. Bake for 18-20 minutes at 375 F
6. When ready remove from the oven and serve

# BANANA MUFFINS

Serves: **8-12**

Prep Time: **10** Minutes

Cook Time: **20** Minutes

Total Time: **30** Minutes

## INGREDIENTS

- 2 eggs
- 1 tablespoon olive oil
- 1 cup milk
- 2 cups whole wheat flour
- 1 tsp baking soda
- ¼ tsp baking soda
- 1 tsp cinnamon
- 1 cup mashed banana

## DIRECTIONS

1. In a bowl combine all dry ingredients
2. In another bowl combine all dry ingredients
3. Combine wet and dry ingredients together

4. Fold in mashed banana and mix well
5. Pour mixture into 8-12 prepared muffin cups, fill 2/3 of the cups
6. Bake for 18-20 minutes at 375 F
7. When ready remove from the oven and serve

## KIWI MUFFINS

Serves: **8-12**

Prep Time: **10** Minutes

Cook Time: **20** Minutes

Total Time: **30** Minutes

### INGREDIENTS

- 2 eggs
- 1 tablespoon olive oil
- 1 cup milk
- 2 cups whole wheat flour
- 1 tsp baking soda
- ¼ tsp baking soda
- 1 tsp cinnamon
- 1 cup mashed kiwi

### DIRECTIONS

1. In a bowl combine all dry ingredients
2. In another bowl combine all dry ingredients
3. Combine wet and dry ingredients together

4. Pour mixture into 8-12 prepared muffin cups, fill 2/3 of the cups
5. Bake for 18-20 minutes at 375 F
6. When ready remove from the oven and serve

# STRAWBERRY MUFFINS

Serves: *8-12*

Prep Time: *10* Minutes

Cook Time: *20* Minutes

Total Time: *30* Minutes

### INGREDIENTS

- 2 eggs
- 1 tablespoon olive oil
- 1 cup milk
- 2 cups whole wheat flour
- 1 tsp baking soda
- ¼ tsp baking soda
- 1 tsp cinnamon
- 1 cup strawberries

### DIRECTIONS

1. In a bowl combine all dry ingredients
2. In another bowl combine all dry ingredients
3. Combine wet and dry ingredients together

4. Pour mixture into 8-12 prepared muffin cups, fill 2/3 of the cups
5. Bake for 18-20 minutes at 375 F
6. When ready remove from the oven and serve

# CRANBERRIES MUFFINS

Serves: **8-12**

Prep Time: **10** Minutes

Cook Time: **20** Minutes

Total Time: **30** Minutes

## INGREDIENTS

- 2 eggs
- 1 tablespoon olive oil
- 1 cup milk
- 2 cups whole wheat flour
- 1 tsp baking soda
- ¼ tsp baking soda
- 1 tsp cinnamon
- 1 cup mashed cranberries

## DIRECTIONS

1. In a bowl combine all dry ingredients
2. In another bowl combine all dry ingredients
3. Combine wet and dry ingredients together

4. Pour mixture into 8-12 prepared muffin cups, fill 2/3 of the cups
5. Bake for 18-20 minutes at 375 F
6. When ready remove from the oven and serve

# MUFFINS

Serves: **8-12**
Prep Time: **10** Minutes
Cook Time: **20** Minutes
Total Time: **30** Minutes

### INGREDIENTS

- 2 eggs
- 1 tablespoon olive oil
- 1 cup milk
- 2 cups whole wheat flour
- 1 tsp baking soda
- ¼ tsp baking soda
- 1 tsp cinnamon

### DIRECTIONS

1. In a bowl combine all dry ingredients
2. In another bowl combine all dry ingredients
3. Combine wet and dry ingredients together

4. Pour mixture into 8-12 prepared muffin cups, fill 2/3 of the cups
5. Bake for 18-20 minutes at 375 F
6. When ready remove from the oven and serve

## CABBAGE OMELETTE

Serves: **1**

Prep Time: **5** Minutes

Cook Time: **10** Minutes

Total Time: **15** Minutes

**INGREDIENTS**

- 2 eggs
- ¼ tsp salt
- ¼ tsp black pepper
- 1 tablespoon olive oil
- ¼ cup cheese
- ½ lb. cucumber
- ¼ tsp basil

**DIRECTIONS**

1. In a bowl combine all ingredients together and mix well
2. In a skillet heat olive oil and pour the egg mixture

3. Cook for 1-2 minutes per side
4. When ready remove omelette from the skillet and serve

## ZUCCHINI OMELETTE

Serves: *1*

Prep Time: *5* Minutes

Cook Time: *10* Minutes

Total Time: *15* Minutes

### INGREDIENTS

- 2 eggs
- ¼ tsp salt
- ¼ tsp black pepper
- 1 tablespoon olive oil
- ¼ cup cheese
- ¼ tsp basil
- 1 cup zucchini

### DIRECTIONS

1. In a bowl combine all ingredients together and mix well
2. In a skillet heat olive oil and pour the egg mixture

3. Cook for 1-2 minutes per side
4. When ready remove omelette from the skillet and serve

# ROMAINE LETTUCE OMELETTE

Serves: **1**

Prep Time: **5** Minutes

Cook Time: **10** Minutes

Total Time: **15** Minutes

### INGREDIENTS

- 2 eggs
- ¼ tsp salt
- ¼ tsp black pepper
- 1 tablespoon olive oil
- ¼ cup cheese
- ¼ tsp basil
- 1 cup romaine lettuce

### DIRECTIONS

1. In a bowl combine all ingredients together and mix well
2. In a skillet heat olive oil and pour the egg mixture

3. Cook for 1-2 minutes per side
4. When ready remove omelette from the skillet and serve

# MUSHROOM OMELETTE

Serves: **1**

Prep Time: **5** Minutes

Cook Time: **10** Minutes

Total Time: **15** Minutes

### INGREDIENTS

- 2 eggs
- ¼ tsp salt
- ¼ tsp black pepper
- 1 tablespoon olive oil
- ¼ cup cheese
- ¼ tsp basil
- 1 cup mushrooms

### DIRECTIONS

1. In a bowl combine all ingredients together and mix well
2. In a skillet heat olive oil and pour the egg mixture

3. Cook for 1-2 minutes per side
4. When ready remove omelette from the skillet and serve

# LEEK OMELETTE

Serves: *1*

Prep Time: *5* Minutes

Cook Time: *10* Minutes

Total Time: *15* Minutes

### INGREDIENTS

- 2 eggs
- ¼ tsp salt
- ¼ tsp black pepper
- 1 tablespoon olive oil
- ¼ cup cheese
- ¼ tsp basil
- 1 cup leeks

### DIRECTIONS

1. In a bowl combine all ingredients together and mix well
2. In a skillet heat olive oil and pour the egg mixture

3. Cook for 1-2 minutes per side
4. When ready remove omelette from the skillet and serve

# COCONUT CEREAL

Serves: **2**

Prep Time: **15** Minutes

Cook Time: **15** Minutes

Total Time: **30** Minutes

### INGREDIENTS

- 1 cup almond flour
- ¼ tsp coconut
- 1 tsp cinnamon
- ¼ tsp salt
- ¼ tsp baking soda
- ¼ tsp vanilla extract
- 1 egg white
- 1 tablespoon olive oil

### DIRECTIONS

1. **Preheat the oven to 375 F**
2. **In a bowl combine baking soda, cinnamon, coconut, almond flour, salt and set aside**

3. In another bowl combine vanilla extract, olive oil and mix well
4. In another bowl whisk the egg white and combine with vanilla extract mixture
5. Add almond flour to the vanilla extract mixture and mix well
6. Transfer dough onto a baking sheet and bake at 375 F for 10-15 minutes
7. When ready remove from the oven and serve

# ZUCCHINI BREAD

Serves: **4**

Prep Time: **10** Minutes

Cook Time: **45** Minutes

Total Time: **55** Minutes

## INGREDIENTS

- 1 zucchini
- 1 cup millet flour
- ½ cup almond flour
- ½ cup buckwheat flour
- 1 tsp baking powder
- ¼ tsp baking soda
- ¼ tsp salt
- ¼ cup almond milk
- 1 tsp apple cider vinegar
- 2 eggs
- ½ cup olive oil

## DIRECTIONS

1. In a bowl combine almond flour, millet flour, buckwheat flour, baking soda, salt and mix well
2. In another bowl combine almond milk and apple cider vinegar
3. In a bowl beats eggs, add almond milk mixture and mix well
4. Add flour mixture to the almond mixture and mix well
5. Fold in zucchini and pour bread batter into pan
6. Bake at 375 F for 40-45 min
7. When ready remove from the oven and serve

# BAKED EGGS WITH ONIONS

Serves: *2*
Prep Time: *10* Minutes
Cook Time: *20* Minutes
Total Time: *30* Minutes

## INGREDIENTS

- 1 tablespoon olive oil
- 1 red bell pepper
- 1 red onion
- 1 cup tomatoes
- ¼ tsp salt
- ¼ tsp pepper
- 2 eggs
- parsley

## DIRECTIONS

1. In a saucepan heat olive oil and sauté peppers and onions until soft

2. Add salt, pepper, tomatoes and cook for 4-5 minutes
3. Remove mixture and form 2 patties
4. Break the eggs into each pattie, top with parsley and place under the broiler for 5-6 minutes
5. When ready remove and serve

# MORNING LOADED SWEET POTATO

Serves: **2**

Prep Time: **15** Minutes

Cook Time: **15** Minutes

Total Time: **30** Minutes

### INGREDIENTS

- 2 sweet potatoes
- 2 tablespoons veggie stock
- ¼ cup cooked rice
- ¼ cup smoked tofu
- 1 onion
- 1 garlic clove
- 1 tsp red pepper flakes
- ¼ tsp cumin
- ¼ tsp oregano

### TOPPING

- 1 tablespoon cheddar cheese

## DIRECTIONS

1. In a microwave bake the potatoes until soft
2. In a skillet sauté onion, red pepper flakes, tofu, oregano, cumin and stir well
3. Add veggie stock, salt and cook for another 4-5 minutes
4. Cut the potatoes lengthwise, mash them and add rice, tofu mixture and sprinkle cheddar cheese on top
5. Bake at 275 F for 8-10 minutes, when ready remove and serve

## *LUNCH*

## ASPARAGUS FRITATTA

Serves: **2**
Prep Time: **10** Minutes
Cook Time: **20** Minutes
Total Time: **30** Minutes

### INGREDIENTS

- ½ lb. asparagus
- 1 tablespoon olive oil
- ½ red onion
- ¼ tsp salt
- 2 oz. cheddar cheese
- 1 garlic clove
- ¼ tsp dill

### DIRECTIONS

1. **In a bowl whisk eggs with salt and cheese**

2. In a frying pan heat olive oil and pour egg mixture
3. Add remaining ingredients and mix well
4. Serve when ready

# FETA CHEESE SALAD DRESSING

Serves: **4**
Prep Time: **10** Minutes
Cook Time: **30** Minutes
Total Time: **40** Minutes

## INGREDIENTS

- ¼ cup olive oil
- ¼ tsp dill weed
- ¼ tsp garlic powder
- ¼ tsp herbs

## DIRECTIONS

1. **In a bowl mix all ingredients and mix well**
2. **Pour dressing into salad and serve**

# BRUSSELS SPROUT SALAD

Serves: **2**
Prep Time: **5** Minutes
Cook Time: **5** Minutes
Total Time: **10** Minutes

### INGREDIENTS

- 1 tablespoon olive oil
- 1 cup shallots
- ½ cup celery
- 1 clove garlic
- 6-8 brussels sprouts
- 1 tablespoon thyme leaves
- herbs

### DIRECTIONS

1. In a bowl mix all ingredients and mix well
2. Serve with dressing

## POTATO SALAD

Serves: **2**

Prep Time: **5** Minutes

Cook Time: **5** Minutes

Total Time: **10** Minutes

### INGREDIENTS

- 1 ½ lb. cooked sweet potatoes
- 2 cups peas
- ½ cup salad dressing
- 1 cup mint leaves
- ½ cup chives

### DIRECTIONS

1. **In a bowl mix all ingredients and mix well**
2. **Serve with dressing**

# CRANBERRY SALAD

Serves: 2
Prep Time: 5 Minutes
Cook Time: 5 Minutes
Total Time: 10 Minutes

## INGREDIENTS

- 1 lb. chickpeas
- 1 cup rocket leaves
- 1 cup cranberries
- 1 cup hazelnuts
- ¼ cup olive oil
- 2 tablespoons lemon juice
- 1 tsp thyme

## DIRECTIONS

1. **In a bowl mix all ingredients and mix well**
2. **Serve with dressing**

## PEA AND LENTIL SALAD

Serves: 2
Prep Time: 5 Minutes
Cook Time: 5 Minutes
Total Time: 10 Minutes

### INGREDIENTS

- 1 cup lentils
- 1 cup green beans
- 1 cup snap peas
- 1 cup red onion
- 2 tablespoons olive oil
- 2 tablespoons lemon juice

### DIRECTIONS

1. **In a bowl mix all ingredients and mix well**
2. **Serve with dressing**

# CHICKEN AND FIG SALAD

Serves: 2
Prep Time: 5 Minutes
Cook Time: 5 Minutes
Total Time: 10 Minutes

## INGREDIENTS

- ¼ cup olive oil
- 1 radicchio
- 1 bunch lettuce leaves
- 1 lb. cooked chicken breast
- 4-5 figs
- 1 cucumber
- 1 cup salad dressing

## DIRECTIONS

1. In a bowl mix all ingredients and mix well
2. Serve with dressing

# BABY CARROT SALAD

Serves: 2
Prep Time: 5 Minutes
Cook Time: 5 Minutes
Total Time: 10 Minutes

## INGREDIENTS

- ¼ cup olive oil
- 1 tablespoon sesame seeds
- 1 tablespoon pumpkin seeds
- 1 lb. baby carrots
- 1 lemon
- 1 tsp mustard
- 1 garlic clove
- ½ lb. rocket leaves
- 1 cup mint leaves

## DIRECTIONS

1. In a bowl mix all ingredients and mix well

2. Serve with dressing

# MUSHROOM & FENNEL SALAD

Serves: **2**

Prep Time: **5** Minutes

Cook Time: **5** Minutes

Total Time: **10** Minutes

### INGREDIENTS

- 1 cup black fungus
- 1 fennel bulb
- ½ lb. mushrooms
- 4 oz. spinach
- ¼ cup mint leaves
- 1 cup salad dressing

### DIRECTIONS

1. **In a bowl mix all ingredients and mix well**
2. **Serve with dressing**

## GREEN BEAN SALAD

Serves: 2

Prep Time: 5 Minutes

Cook Time: 5 Minutes

Total Time: 10 Minutes

### INGREDIENTS

- 1 lb. cooked green beans
- 1 tsp mustard
- ¼ cup basil leaves
- 1 cup salad dressing

### DIRECTIONS

1. **In a bowl mix all ingredients and mix well**
2. **Serve with dressing**

# WATERCRESS AND PEAR SALAD

Serves: **2**
Prep Time: **5** Minutes
Cook Time: **5** Minutes
Total Time: **10** Minutes

### INGREDIENTS

- 1 pear
- 4-5 slices pancetta
- 1 red onion
- 1 bunch watercress
- ½ lb. goat cheese
- ¼ bunch parsley

### DIRECTIONS

1. **In a bowl mix all ingredients and mix well**
2. **Serve with dressing**

# WATERCRESS FRITATTA

Serves: **2**

Prep Time: **10** Minutes

Cook Time: **20** Minutes

Total Time: **30** Minutes

## INGREDIENTS

- ½ lb. watercress
- 1 tablespoon olive oil
- ½ red onion
- ¼ tsp salt
- 2 oz. cheddar cheese
- 1 garlic clove
- ¼ tsp dill

## DIRECTIONS

1. In a bowl whisk eggs with salt and cheese
2. In a frying pan heat olive oil and pour egg mixture
3. Add remaining ingredients and mix well

4. Serve when ready

# KALE FRITATTA

Serves: **2**

Prep Time: **10** Minutes

Cook Time: **20** Minutes

Total Time: **30** Minutes

### INGREDIENTS

- 1 cup kale
- 1 tablespoon olive oil
- ½ red onion
- ¼ tsp salt
- 2 oz. cheddar cheese
- 1 garlic clove
- ¼ tsp dill

### DIRECTIONS

1. In a skillet sauté kale until tender
2. In a bowl whisk eggs with salt and cheese
3. In a frying pan heat olive oil and pour egg mixture

4. Add remaining ingredients and mix well
5. When ready serve with sautéed kale

# TOMATO FRITATTA

Serves: **2**

Prep Time: **10** Minutes

Cook Time: **20** Minutes

Total Time: **30** Minutes

### INGREDIENTS

- ½ lb. tomato
- 1 tablespoon olive oil
- ½ red onion
- ¼ tsp salt
- 2 oz. parmesan cheese
- 1 garlic clove
- ¼ tsp dill

### DIRECTIONS

1. In a bowl whisk eggs with salt and parmesan cheese
2. In a frying pan heat olive oil and pour egg mixture

3. Add remaining ingredients and mix well
4. Serve when ready

# BROCCOLI FRITATTA

Serves: **2**

Prep Time: **10** Minutes

Cook Time: **20** Minutes

Total Time: **30** Minutes

## INGREDIENTS

- 1 cup broccoli
- 1 tablespoon olive oil
- ½ red onion
- ¼ tsp salt
- 2 oz. cheddar cheese
- 1 garlic clove
- ¼ tsp dill

## DIRECTIONS

1. In a skillet sauté broccoli until tender
2. In a bowl whisk eggs with salt and cheese
3. In a frying pan heat olive oil and pour egg mixture

4. Add remaining ingredients and mix well
5. When ready serve with sautéed broccoli

# MEDITERRANENA BUDDA BOWL

Serves: **1**

Prep Time: **10** Minutes

Cook Time: **10** Minutes

Total Time: **20** Minutes

### INGREDIENTS

- 1 zucchini
- ¼ tsp oregano
- Salt
- 1 cup cooked quinoa
- 1 cup spinach
- 1 cup mixed greens
- ½ cup red pepper
- ¼ cup cucumber
- ¼ cup tomatoes
- parsley
- Tahini dressing

DIRECTIONS

1. In a skillet heat olive oil olive and sauté zucchini until soft and sprinkle oregano over zucchini
2. In a bowl add the rest of ingredients and toss to combine
3. Add fried zucchini and mix well
4. Pour over tahini dressing, mix well and serve

# VEGAN CURRY

Serves: **4**

Prep Time: **10** Minutes

Cook Time: **20** Minutes

Total Time: **30** Minutes

## INGREDIENTS

- 1 tablespoon olive oil
- ¼ cup onion
- 2 stalks celery
- 1 garlic clove
- ¼ tsp coriander
- ¼ tsp cumin
- ¼ tsp turmeric
- ¼ tsp red pepper flakes
- 1 cauliflower
- 1 zucchini
- 2 tomatoes
- 1 tsp salt
- 1 cup vegetable broth

- 1 handful of baby spinach
- 1 tablespoon almonds
- 1 tablespoon cilantro

## DIRECTIONS

1. In a skillet heat olive oil and sauté celery, garlic and onions for 4-5 minutes or until vegetables are tender
2. Add cumin, spices, coriander, cumin, turmeric red pepper flakes stir to combine and cook for another 1-2 minutes
3. Add zucchini, cauliflower, tomatoes, broth, spinach, water and simmer on low heat for 15-20 minutes
4. Add remaining ingredients and simmer for another 4-5 minutes
5. Garnish curry and serve

# CAULIFLOWER WITH ROSEMARY

Serves: 2
Prep Time: 5 Minutes
Cook Time: 15 Minutes
Total Time: 20 Minutes

## INGREDIENTS

- 1 cauliflower
- 1 tablespoon rosemary
- 1 cup vegetable stock
- 2 garlic cloves
- salt

## DIRECTIONS

1. In a saucepan add cauliflower, stock and bring to a boil for 12-15 minutes
2. Blend cauliflower until smooth, add garlic, salt, rosemary and blend again
3. When ready pour in a bowl and serve

# BRUSSELS SPROUTS

Serves: *2*
Prep Time: *10* Minutes
Cook Time: *20* Minutes
Total Time: *30* Minutes

### INGREDIENTS

- 1 tablespoon olive oil
- 2 shallots
- 2 cloves garlic
- 1 lb. brussels sprouts
- 1 cup vegetable stock
- 4 springs thyme
- ¼ cup pine nuts

### DIRECTIONS

1. **In a pan heat olive oil and cook shallots until tender**
2. **Add garlic, sprouts, thyme, stock and cook for another 4-5 minutes**

3. Cover and cook for another 10-12 minutes or until sprouts are soft
4. When ready add pine nuts and serve

# MOROCCAN STIR FRY

Serves: *2*

Prep Time: *10* Minutes

Cook Time: *20* Minutes

Total Time: *30* Minutes

## INGREDIENTS

- ¼ cup onion
- 1 clove garlic
- 1 lb. ground turkey
- 1 tsp all spice
- 1 tsp cumin
- 1 tsp salt
- 2 cups cabbage
- 1 tablespoon mint
- 1 red bell pepper
- Zest of 1 lemon
- 1 tablespoon lemon juice
- plain yogurt
- pint leaves

DIRECTIONS

1. In a skillet heat olive oil and sauté garlic, onion until soft
2. Add cumin, pepper, salt, all spice, ground turkey and sauté for 8-10 minutes
3. Add cabbage, red bell pepper, pint leaves, lemon zest and sauté for 4-5 minutes
4. When ready garnish with mint leaves, yogurt and serve

## *DINNER*

## SIMPLE PIZZA RECIPE

Serves: **6-8**

Prep Time: **10** Minutes

Cook Time: **15** Minutes

Total Time: **25** Minutes

### INGREDIENTS

- 1 pizza crust
- ½ cup tomato sauce
- ¼ black pepper
- 1 cup pepperoni slices
- 1 cup mozzarella cheese
- 1 cup olives

### DIRECTIONS

1. **Spread tomato sauce on the pizza crust**
2. **Place all the toppings on the pizza crust**
3. **Bake the pizza at 425 F for 12-15 minutes**

4. When ready remove pizza from the oven and serve

# ZUCCHINI PIZZA

Serves: **6-8**

Prep Time: **10** Minutes

Cook Time: **15** Minutes

Total Time: **25** Minutes

### INGREDIENTS

- 1 pizza crust
- ½ cup tomato sauce
- ¼ black pepper
- 1 cup zucchini slices
- 1 cup mozzarella cheese
- 1 cup olives

### DIRECTIONS

1. Spread tomato sauce on the pizza crust
2. Place all the toppings on the pizza crust
3. Bake the pizza at 425 F for 12-15 minutes
4. When ready remove pizza from the oven and serve

# CAULIFLOWER RECIPE

Serves: **6-8**

Prep Time: **10** Minutes

Cook Time: **15** Minutes

Total Time: **25** Minutes

### INGREDIENTS

- 1 pizza crust
- ½ cup tomato sauce
- ¼ black pepper
- 1 cup cauliflower
- 1 cup mozzarella cheese
- 1 cup olives

### DIRECTIONS

1. Spread tomato sauce on the pizza crust
2. Place all the toppings on the pizza crust
3. Bake the pizza at 425 F for 12-15 minutes
4. When ready remove pizza from the oven and serve

## BROCCOLI RECIPE

Serves: **6-8**

Prep Time: **10** Minutes

Cook Time: **15** Minutes

Total Time: **25** Minutes

### INGREDIENTS

- 1 pizza crust
- ½ cup tomato sauce
- ¼ black pepper
- 1 cup broccoli
- 1 cup mozzarella cheese
- 1 cup olives

### DIRECTIONS

1. Spread tomato sauce on the pizza crust
2. Place all the toppings on the pizza crust
3. Bake the pizza at 425 F for 12-15 minutes
4. When ready remove pizza from the oven and serve

# TOMATOES & HAM PIZZA

Serves: **6-8**
Prep Time: **10** Minutes
Cook Time: **15** Minutes
Total Time: **25** Minutes

### INGREDIENTS

- 1 pizza crust
- ½ cup tomato sauce
- ¼ black pepper
- 1 cup pepperoni slices
- 1 cup tomatoes
- 6-8 ham slices
- 1 cup mozzarella cheese
- 1 cup olives

### DIRECTIONS

1. Spread tomato sauce on the pizza crust
2. Place all the toppings on the pizza crust
3. Bake the pizza at 425 F for 12-15 minutes

4. **When ready remove pizza from the oven and serve**

# LEEK SOUP

Serves: *4*
Prep Time: *10* Minutes
Cook Time: *20* Minutes
Total Time: *30* Minutes

## INGREDIENTS

- 1 tablespoon olive oil
- 1 lb. leek
- ¼ red onion
- ½ cup all-purpose flour
- ¼ tsp salt
- ¼ tsp pepper
- 1 can vegetable broth
- 1 cup heavy cream

## DIRECTIONS

1. **In a saucepan heat olive oil and sauté onion until tender**

2. Add remaining ingredients to the saucepan and bring to a boil
3. When all the vegetables are tender transfer to a blender and blend until smooth
4. Pour soup into bowls, garnish with parsley and serve

# ZUCCHINI SOUP

Serves: *4*
Prep Time: *10* Minutes
Cook Time: *20* Minutes
Total Time: *30* Minutes

### INGREDIENTS

- **1 tablespoon olive oil**
- **1 lb. zucchini**
- **¼ red onion**
- **½ cup all-purpose flour**
- **¼ tsp salt**
- **¼ tsp pepper**
- **1 can vegetable broth**
- **1 cup heavy cream**

### DIRECTIONS

1. **In a saucepan heat olive oil and sauté zucchini until tender**

2. Add remaining ingredients to the saucepan and bring to a boil
3. When all the vegetables are tender transfer to a blender and blend until smooth
4. Pour soup into bowls, garnish with parsley and serve

# RUTABAGA SOUP

Serves: **4**

Prep Time: **10** Minutes

Cook Time: **20** Minutes

Total Time: **30** Minutes

### INGREDIENTS

- 1 tablespoon olive oil
- 1 lb. rutabaga
- ¼ red onion
- ½ cup all-purpose flour
- ¼ tsp salt
- ¼ tsp pepper
- 1 can vegetable broth
- 1 cup heavy cream

### DIRECTIONS

1. **In a saucepan heat olive oil and sauté onion until tender**

2. Add remaining ingredients to the saucepan and bring to a boil
3. When all the vegetables are tender transfer to a blender and blend until smooth
4. Pour soup into bowls, garnish with parsley and serve

## CARROT SOUP

Serves: **4**
Prep Time: **10** Minutes
Cook Time: **20** Minutes
Total Time: **30** Minutes

### INGREDIENTS

- 1 tablespoon olive oil
- 1 lb. carrots
- ¼ red onion
- ½ cup all-purpose flour
- ¼ tsp salt
- ¼ tsp pepper
- 1 can vegetable broth
- 1 cup heavy cream

### DIRECTIONS

1. **In a saucepan heat olive oil and sauté carrots until tender**

2. Add remaining ingredients to the saucepan and bring to a boil
3. When all the vegetables are tender transfer to a blender and blend until smooth
4. Pour soup into bowls, garnish with parsley and serve

# YAMS SOUP

Serves: **4**
Prep Time: **10** Minutes
Cook Time: **20** Minutes
Total Time: **30** Minutes

### INGREDIENTS

- 1 tablespoon olive oil
- 1 lb. yams
- ¼ red onion
- ½ cup all-purpose flour
- ¼ tsp salt
- ¼ tsp pepper
- 1 can vegetable broth
- 1 cup heavy cream

### DIRECTIONS

1. **In a saucepan heat olive oil and sauté onion until tender**

2. Add remaining ingredients to the saucepan and bring to a boil
3. When all the vegetables are tender transfer to a blender and blend until smooth
4. Pour soup into bowls, garnish with parsley and serve

## *SMOOTHIES*

## TANGERINE SMOOTHIE

Serves: *1*

Prep Time: *5* Minutes

Cook Time: *5* Minutes

Total Time: *10* Minutes

### INGREDIENTS

- 2 tangerines
- 1 cup pineapple
- 1 banana
- 1 cup ice

### DIRECTIONS

1. **In a blender place all ingredients and blend until smooth**
2. **Pour smoothie in a glass and serve**

# PEANUT BUTTER SMOOTHIE

Serves: *1*

Prep Time: *5* Minutes

Cook Time: *5* Minutes

Total Time: *10* Minutes

## INGREDIENTS

- 1 cup strawberries
- 1 banana
- 2 tablespoons peanut butter

## DIRECTIONS

1. **In a blender place all ingredients and blend until smooth**
2. **Pour smoothie in a glass and serve**

# CARROT SMOOTHIE

Serves: *1*

Prep Time: *5* Minutes

Cook Time: *5* Minutes

Total Time: *10* Minutes

### INGREDIENTS

- 1 carrot
- 1 mango
- 2 tablespoons coconut flakes

### DIRECTIONS

1. **In a blender place all ingredients and blend until smooth**
2. **Pour smoothie in a glass and serve**

## GINGER SMOOTHIE

Serves: *1*

Prep Time: *5* Minutes

Cook Time: *5* Minutes

Total Time: *10* Minutes

### INGREDIENTS

- 2 cups pineapple
- 2 tablespoons lime juice
- 1-pice ginger

### DIRECTIONS

1. **In a blender place all ingredients and blend until smooth**
2. **Pour smoothie in a glass and serve**

# KALE SMOOTHIE

Serves: *1*

Prep Time: *5* Minutes

Cook Time: *5* Minutes

Total Time: *10* Minutes

## INGREDIENTS

- 1 cup kale
- 1 cup cherries
- 1 cup blueberries

## DIRECTIONS

1. In a blender place all ingredients and blend until smooth
2. Pour smoothie in a glass and serve

## MANGO SMOOTHIE

Serves: *1*

Prep Time: *5* Minutes

Cook Time: *5* Minutes

Total Time: *10* Minutes

### INGREDIENTS

- 1 cup mango
- 1 cup cherries
- 1 cup Greek yogurt

### DIRECTIONS

1. **In a blender place all ingredients and blend until smooth**
2. **Pour smoothie in a glass and serve**

# CHIA SMOOTHIE

Serves: *1*
Prep Time: *5* Minutes
Cook Time: *5* Minutes
Total Time: *10* Minutes

### INGREDIENTS

- 1 cup raspberries
- 1 banana
- 1 chia seeds

### DIRECTIONS

1. In a blender place all ingredients and blend until smooth
2. Pour smoothie in a glass and serve

# CRANBERRY SMOOTHIE

Serves: *1*
Prep Time: *5* Minutes
Cook Time: *5* Minutes
Total Time: *10* Minutes

### INGREDIENTS

- 1 cup raspberries
- 1 banana
- 1 tsp chia seeds
- 1 cup cherries
- 1 cup ice

### DIRECTIONS

1. **In a blender place all ingredients and blend until smooth**
2. **Pour smoothie in a glass and serve**

# PINEAPPLE & SPINACH SMOOTHIE

Serves: **1**

Prep Time: **5** Minutes

Cook Time: **5** Minutes

Total Time: **10** Minutes

### INGREDIENTS

- 1 cup pineapple
- 1 cup cranberries
- ½ cup spinach
- ½ cup coconut water
- 1 cup ice

### DIRECTIONS

1. **In a blender place all ingredients and blend until smooth**
2. **Pour smoothie in a glass and serve**

# BLUEBERRY SMOOTHIE

Serves: *1*
Prep Time: *5* Minutes
Cook Time: *5* Minutes
Total Time: *10* Minutes

### INGREDIENTS

- 1 banana
- ½ pear
- ½ apple
- 1 cup blueberries
- ½ cup soy milk

### DIRECTIONS

1. In a blender place all ingredients and blend until smooth
2. Pour smoothie in a glass and serve

**THANK YOU FOR READING THIS BOOK!**

Made in the USA
Las Vegas, NV
21 December 2021

39142477R00062